3 1994 01319 2205

SANTA ANA PUBLIC LIBRARY

AR PTS: 0.5

D0773754

HORSEPOWER

MONSTER TRUCKS

by Matt Doeden

Reading Consultant:

Barbara J. Fox

Reading Specialist

North Carolina State University

Capstone

J 796.7 DOE
Doeden, Matt
Monster trucks

CENTRAL

$19.93

31994013192205

Blazers is published by Capstone Press,
151 Good Counsel Drive, P.O. Box 669, Mankato, Minnesota 56002.
www.capstonepress.com

Copyright © 2005 by Capstone Press. All rights reserved.
No part of this publication may be reproduced in whole or in part, or stored in a retrieval system, or transmitted in any form or by any means, electronic, mechanical, photocopying, recording, or otherwise, without written permission of the publisher. For information regarding permission, write to Capstone Press, 151 Good Counsel Drive, P.O. Box 669, Dept. R, Mankato, Minnesota 56002.
Printed in the United States of America

Library of Congress Cataloging-in-Publication Data
Doeden, Matt.
    Monster trucks / by Matt Doeden.
    p. cm.—(Blazers. horsepower)
    Includes bibliographical references and index.
    ISBN 0-7368-2732-3 (hardcover)
    ISBN 0-7368-5218-2 (paperback)
    1. Monster trucks—Juvenile literature. [1. Monster trucks. 2. Trucks.]
    I. Title. II. Series: Horsepower (Mankato, Minn.)
TL230.15.D64 2005
796.7—dc22   2003026084

Summary: Describes monster trucks, their origin, design, and competitions.

Editorial Credits
James Anderson, editor; Jason Knudson, designer; Jo Miller, photo researcher; Eric Kudalis, product planning editor

Photo Credits
Action Images/Dave & Bev Huntoon 11, 12, 13, 15 (both), 16, 17, 18, 19 (both), 20–21, 24–25, 26, 27 (both), 28–29
SportsChrome, Inc./Ross F. Dettman, cover, 5, 6–7, 8–9 (all), 23

The publisher does not endorse products whose logos may appear on objects in images in this book.

1 2 3 4 5 6 09 08 07 06 05 04

TABLE OF CONTENTS

THE CRUSH

The monster truck Black Stallion is about to crush an old bus. Fans scream and cheer. The truck's noisy engine is louder than the crowd.

Black Stallion bounces above
the bus. All four tires are in the air.
The fans yell even louder!

With more than 10,000 pounds
(4,500 kilograms), Black Stallion comes
down with a thud. The driver gets out
and waves to the crowd.

BIG TIRES

Bob Chandler built the first
monster truck in the 1970s.
He named it Bigfoot.

Monster truck wheels were first
used for huge tractors. Extra large
axles hold the wheels.

Monster truck tires are more than 5 feet (1.5 meters) tall. They cost about $1,500 each.

Axle

MONSTER TRUCK POWER

Monster trucks have powerful engines. The trucks can go up to 70 miles (113 kilometers) an hour.

Shocks

Monster trucks have strong shocks. These springs allow the trucks to land safely from 100-foot (30-meter) jumps.

BLAZER FACT

Monster trucks cost
more than $100,000.

Roll cages protect drivers during crashes. Officials use a shut-off switch to turn off the engine if the driver can't reach the key.

BLAZER FACT

Most monster trucks have doors in the floor for the driver to crawl out safely.

Roll Cage

MONSTER TRUCK DIAGRAM

Shocks

Tire

Roll cage

Engine

MONSTER TRUCKS IN ACTION

Monster truck drivers
enter car-crushing events.
The trucks drive over old cars.

Some drivers race their trucks.
They speed through turns and over
jumps. They also race over old cars.

During crushing events, monster trucks only go about 30 miles (48 kilometers) an hour.

Freestyle monster truck driving is another event. Drivers do wheelies, jumps, donuts, and other tricks.

GRAVE DIGGER
JUMPS OVER OLD CARS.

GLOSSARY

axle (AK-suhl)—a rod in the center of the wheels; wheels turn around an axle.

donut (DOH-nuht)—a trick in which a monster truck spins in a circle

official (uh-FISH-uhl)—the person who enforces the rules of a monster truck event

shocks (SHOKS)—springs that help monster trucks bounce after a landing; shocks is short for shock absorbers.

tractor (TRAK-tur)—a powerful vehicle used for farm and construction work

READ MORE

Maurer, Tracy Nelson. *Monster Trucks.* Roaring Rides. Vero Beach, Fla.: Rourke, 2003.

Nelson, Kristin L. *Monster Trucks.* Pull Ahead Books. Minneapolis: Lerner, 2003.

Schaefer, A. R. *Monster Trucks.* Wild Rides!. Mankato, Minn.: Capstone Press, 2002.

INTERNET SITES

FactHound offers a safe, fun way to find Internet sites related to this book. All of the sites on FactHound have been researched by our staff.

Here's how:

1. Visit *www.facthound.com*
2. Type in this special code **0736827323** for age-appropriate sites. Or enter a search word related to this book for a more general search.
3. Click on the **Fetch It** button.

FactHound will fetch the best sites for you!

INDEX